What To Believe About God, the Bible & Christ Jesus

This is answered in the Bible from 1 Peter 3:15 "But sanctify the Lord God in your hearts; and be ready always to give an answer to every man that asketh you a reason of the hope that is in you with meekness and fear:" (KJV) that we should be able to give an account for the reason of our great hope in our Lord and Savior Christ Jesus.

As for me, It is because I, like Ignatius truly know that Christ is Lord because I've been born again by HIS holy spirit. My life has been turned upside down and inside out causing me to be turned from gross darkness into HIS marvelous saving light.

Because I have had so many real encounters with the Holy Spirit and Christ Jesus this is the reason why my faith has been so deeply rooted in HIM and HIS Word. When one has experienced such a life changing watershed moment in their life they cannot help but to be a living testament as to the event when their life changes from the darkness of sin to the light of the gospel life of Christ Jesus and HIS ways as taught in scripture. And we are admonished all through scriptures to teach others what we have heard and to disciple them.

Reply; The word of God is everything to me. But it hasn't always been that way. It only became that way the past 13 years of my life. My best friend suggested that I set aside a time to spend with God each morning. She taught me the priestly benediction from Numbers 6:22-27.

And from there I just began digging in HIS word more often. And God began speaking to me about events and circumstances in my life so I began relying on HIS word a lot more for my guidance. I just love HIS word so much that I carry it with me everywhere I go.

As for the reason that I personally believe; I became born again in 1988. From that moment I went from being an atheist to being born again and it was kind of like Saul of Tarsus being transformed on the road to Damaskus because I felt that everything that I had learned up to that day was false and once I became born again I felt as if I had been enlightened to truth.

Why It Is Important To Know What To Believe & Why To Believe It

We are instructed in 2 Timothy 4:2 "Preach the word; be instant in season, out of season; reprove, rebuke, exhort with all longsuffering and doctrine."(KJV) and 1 Peter 3:15 "But sanctify the Lord God in your hearts; and be ready always to give an answer to every man that asketh you a reason of the hope that is in you with meekness and fear:" (KJV) this would answer the "Why" one would proclaim his/her faith to another.

The "What" one would believe would determine the amount of passion one would proclaim such a life changing view to another. The verse in 2 Timothy 4:2 "Preach the word; be instant in season, out of season; reprove, rebuke, exhort with all longsuffering and doctrine." (KJV) and that clarifies to me that I should know "WHY" I believe and "What" I believe.

Timothy says we have to know what we are to say about what we believe and why we believe it. As Ben Gutierrez says "Passionate Pleading with Precision and Patience."

Reply Comment: I was born again 23 years ago. Until then, I guess you could say that I was really an atheist. At the very moment I became born again it was as if everything that I had ever learned or knew from the time I was born was proven to be false. My life was turned inside out and upside down.

Until then I thought I knew everything that one could know about this life but I found out that I had been believing a lie my entire life until the moment that I was born again. It truly was as if I had a Saul to Paul conversion on the road to Damaskus.

WorldView

I. Worldview is a set of standards in which one looks at the events, circumstances, relationships and all that one encounters throughout the life process. Worldview can vary from one time period in one's life to the next. For example,

before I was saved I viewed the bible as man's ways to control society. A policing system that was spread out on mankind to cut down on crimes and to control communities.

II. My worldview of scripture and life in its entirety changed drastically after I was born again to the point that now everything that comes in or goes out of my life is scrutinized finely by the laws of the Spirit and by God's word.

HIS word is used as a type of sifter to weigh every event, everything, and everyone in my life now. I have done so for many years. I haven't always been perfect but when I missed the mark it was easy to see through the scripture.

Origin; As Christians we did not come to being as the Islāmic Faith believes that we were created gradually in stages and from a liquid substance. Man was created from dust by the hands of God [Genesis 2:7 "And the Lord God formed man of the dust of the ground and breathed into his nostrils the breath of life; and man became a living soul"] just like when Jesus went to heal the eyes of one blind man and HE bent down, picked up some clay of the earth, mixed it with HIS spittle and rubbed it into the mans eyes to make them new again or to heal them. [John 9:6 "When HE had thus spoken, HE had spat on the ground and made clay from spittle, and HE anointed the eyes of the blind man with clay"]

Identity; My cat, my bunny or my bamboo plant are not equal with me or with any mankind. God made mankind an original. We are a one of a kind made in HIS image and we have a soul. [Genesis 1:27 "So God created man in HIS own image, in the image of God created HE him; male and female created HE them."]

And God even created us to be esteemed higher than HIS heavenly host; the angels. [Psalm 8:5 "For you have made him a little lower than the angels and have crowned him with glory and honor."]

Purpose; If Christians suffer for Christ in this life time for nothing, for no purpose than would they not be the first to commit suicide. If all the rejection from society, the being an outcast on trains where many are drunken or under the influence to ball games that we have to ride along as passengers with though we wish not to be in danger of any unruly person under the influence.

To have been looked down upon many times and accused of judging others when we took a stand for life to and a stand against abortion or gay marriage. [Luke 10:19 "He that heareth you heareth me; and he that despiseth you despiseth me; and he that despiseth me despiseth he that sent me."]

If a Christian had no purpose, no mandate by divine revelation, no call of God on his or her life then what would be any purpose of the suffering that this life brings to so many? [1 Corinthians 15:19 "If in this life only we have hope in Christ, in this life we are of all men to be pitied."]

Morality; Morals and Ethics can mean many things. The spirit of the Lord sometimes requires more of Christians then the law of God required of the Jews. Some Christians used to wear the bracelets "WWJD" that stood for "What Would Jesus Do" and this is a good place to start if one really wants to apply a Christian Worldview to every area of their lives.

What would Jesus do if HE were passing a hurt or weak person lying on the side of the road? [Luke 10:34 "He went to him, and bound up his wounds, pouring in oil and wine, and set him on his own beast, and brought him to an inn, and took care of him."
Or what should we do about abortion when raging rivers of blood and baby body parts are rushing through our cities and states throughout this nation? We must take a stand against abortion!
God says HE hates the shedding of innocent blood when HE tells us the seven things that he abhors in the book of Proverbs. [Proverbs 6:16-17 Six things doth the Lord hate; yea, seven are an abomination to HIM: A proud look, a lying tongue, and hands that shed innocent blood, An heart that deviseth wicked imaginations, feet that be swift in running to mischief, A false witness that speaketh lies, and he that soweth discord among the brethren."]

Destiny: As with purpose if there is no reason to suffer while living for Christ to have a hope of being rewarded in Heaven for what we endured for Christ while here on earth then for what reason would anyone have to serve HIM?

God promises us that one day we will have final victory

over the adversary of our soul; the great Beelzebub, the great dragon, Satan, the devil who is the headship of hates or hell.

[Revelations 20:1 "And I saw an angel come down from heaven having the key of the bottomless pit and a great chain in his hand, And he laid hold on the dragon, that old serpent, which is the Devil and Satan.

And bound him up for a thousand years, And cast him into the bottomless pit, and shut him up, and set a seal upon him, that he should deceive the nations no more, till the thousand years should be fulfilled and after that he must be loosed for a little season."]

III. a. My biblical worldview affects the way that I vote in a national election because I go to http://votesmart.org/ and I order voting guides (especially on presidential campaigns) and then I distribute them while I am shopping at the grocery store in the parking lot while people are headed to their cars or going into the stores. I pass them out anywhere that I can.

And if it is a particular issue that I know is relevant and important to this campaign then I will gain as much information as I can and I will say a little something to the people while I am handing them the literature. One year when president Bush was running for office I would describe what a partial birth abortion process consisted of.

[Proverbs 6:16-17 Six things doth the Lord hate; yea, seven are an abomination to HIM: A proud look, a lying tongue, and hands that shed innocent blood, An heart that deviseth wicked imaginations, feet that be swift in running to mischief, A false witness that speaketh lies, and he that soweth discord among the brethren."]

President Bush won that year and it was in South Florida

where I was able to distribute the voter guides and vote smart literature. You can also sign up to be a volunteer at the Christian Coalition where they will provide you with your own profile and widgets.
http://www.cc.org/voter_guides

I find the voter guides a bit more user friendly for those who don't have a lot of time to research a particular candidate. I support candidates who are pro life only and who want to protect the constitution when it comes to traditional marriage between one man and one woman.

I don't think we should support those who are destroying our planet at rates so fast that we will need a miracle to reverse the damages done by the oil industry to our oceans, our lands, our air quality and our planet. We are instructed in God's word that it is our responsibility to take dominion over the earth and care for it.

[Genesis 1:28 "And God blessed them, and God said unto them, Be fruitful, and multiply and replenish the earth and subdue it; and have dominion over the fish of the sea and the foul of the air, and over every living thing that moveth upon the earth"] And [Genesis 2:15 "And then the Lord God took the man, and put him into the garden of Eden to dress it and to keep it"]

b. My Career Choice is also based on my Christian Worldview after a revelatory dream that the Lord gave me(see more here http://kimig.tripod.com/thedream/)five years after I was deemed permanently disabled in 2000. It was in October of 2005 and I had just lost my home of seven years. It was the first home that I had since the kids and I lost our five bedroom home in Clinton, MS. Granted it this was only a ghetto apartment but I was happy and I had a five year ministry to the youth there in Tarpon

Springs, Florida where I would take about 100 children to three different local churches between Tarpon Springs, FL and Clearwater, Florida. I also taught them free piano lessons, took them to the beach weekly and baptized many of them nine months of the year from 2000 to 2005. See more here;
http://kimig.tripod.com/kimgerredtranscript/kim-gerred-nelson-s-youth-ministry.html

Many of the kids were saved at my front door where I had a Jewish Mezuzah and I wanted all who entered to touch it while reciting the Jewish blessing "The Lord my God is one" Inside the Mezuzah was the scroll of the ten commandments and dozens of prayer requests that I had placed in there. That October the Lord spoke clearly to me in a dream that HIS purpose for my life was politics. I thought about all the other bad stuff that had happened but I knew that God had spoke clearly and that nothing could oppose HIS will (not even my disabilities of which most were mobility) for me to run in politics.

HE had also been speaking to me from 2000 through 2005 from [Isaiah 60 "For the nation and kingdom that will not serve thee shall perish, yea, those nations shall be utterly wasted."] Then I thought about what that would mean in relation to politics. And how God had been speaking to me from [Psalm 18:43 also found in 2 Samuel 22 "Thou hast delivered me from the striving of the people; and thou hast made me the head of the heathen: a people whom I have not known shall serve me."]

A lot has happened since then, I spent from October 2005 until January of 2008 homeless as a very sick person. That dream was all I had to go by to keep hope alive. There were hundreds of others of homeless too as I left Tarpon Springs, Fl just two weeks after Hurricane Katrina had left hundreds of thousands homeless in September of 2005 including in my home state of Mississippi.

So housing was slim to none for all of us. I stayed on my old church Sunday school floor for about a year, slept on a missionaries floor for three months all the while I stayed busy about my father's business of saving souls by the distribution of the publication of the gospel and telling people about the Lord. But in the back of my mind I always kept the dream alive. I registered to vote in every place that I moved to and one time I even ran a small campaign for a town I had only stepped in for the first time in my life.

The campaign began 3 months after I moved to town. I was running against an eight term mayor who was a former Navy vet and six weeks after I jumped in the campaign the mayor's wife was killed in an auto accident. But I got my feet wet, a good newspaper article was written about me and I won 18% of the vote and I was a little newcomer to town. I was still very ill and had to have a major oral surgery the following year but nothing has stopped me from believing what God has spoken HE is able to do. I will leave the timing and the campaign in HIS hands now. And I will just keep doing what I know will help HIS cause.

The Gospel Message

 Some of the ways that the Christian Gospel is perceived in our culture is that a person needs to be good enough to go to heaven. Some churches who even believe in most of the Bible do not believe that they will be accepted unless their good works are enough to prove they love God. Others believe that their good works is what will get them to heaven.

And still others who have not even come to the Lord yet are too afraid to come to God because they think they are going to have to stop doing what they are doing and change the way they live before they can get saved. None of those beliefs are true.

The Bible says in Ephesians 2:8 That it is not by works that we are saved but by Grace through our Lord and savior Jesus Christ. And in Titus 3:5 Says there is no way to get saved through good thoughts or good deeds. And it also says in Romans 3:23 "For all have sinned and come short of the Glory of God." And Isaiah 64:6 Says that our righteousness is as filthy rags.

Some specific moral reasons that people may reject the Christian Gospel is again because they might not think that they are as bad as murders, adulterers or thieves. They might not think there is anything wrong with them if they compare their selves to other people. But if they would compare their selves to God's holiness then they would know that they will never measure up no matter how good they are.

Some specific emotional reasons that people may reject the Christian Gospel is pride. They may think they are not bad people at all if they are comparing themselves to another person rather than to God.

Some intellectual reasons that people may reject the Christian Gospel is that they know that their sins have separated them from a Holy God. And in knowing this some have tried to solve this problem on their own by their own good works rather than doing it God's way through HIS SON Christ Jesus.

A Christian with Global Apologetic knowledge of the people, group or person that has not accepted the Christian Gospel message can lead them to the truth with a few verses about good works not being good enough then tell them about 1 Corinthians 15:1-4 about Jesus dying for their sins, HE was buried and raised again back to life, tell them that if they call unto the Lord they will be saved according to Romans 10:13, Then lastly they must confess with their mouths that Jesus is Lord of their lives and they must believe in their heart Jesus died for their sins and is raised again then they shall be saved according to Romans 10:9

The Problem of Evil

God could have created us to be robots that do exactly what HE wanted us to do but HE would have been so bored. No one would have their own individuality, no conscious to choose from right or wrong and no need for HIS chastisement to show us that HE loves us. John14:15 says "If you love me you, will keep my commandments" and just like with our earthly parents, we are given the choice to obey them or to rebel. Sometimes there are consequences and other times our bad behavior can seemingly go unpunished by our parents.

But as in all areas of life, God has set order to everything. HE chastens those HE loves. "The fear of the Lord is the beginning of all wisdom" Proverbs 9:10 and in Job 28:28 we are told that "the fear of the Lord--that is wisdom and to shun evil is understanding." God gave us a choice. Without evil we would not have the benefit of the choice. Nor would we have the benefit of the blessing because blessing comes by obeying HIS word. See Psalm 119:5 and Ecclesiastes 8:11-12 about how righteousness brings protection and blessing.

We cannot blame all bad things on God. God is only the author of life, good and blessing. If anything bad happens like earthquakes, wars, famines... those are all a result of the fall of Adam. They are a result of sin in this world.

I live in California where we have lots of earthquakes. I also love Science. Take a ball of soft clay then let all the moisture dry out of it like the effects that a drought would have then watch it start to crumble and crack. God promises when HIS people own and possess the land that HE will care for the land and send water in its season. He says this all through Leviticus and Deuteronomy that HIS people have to care for the land like HE tells them to. HE also tells us that HE will send the blessing upon the land of HIS care in Genesis 27:28.

If a drought comes the clay, the earth dries up and shrinks. It becomes condensed in size. Add water or rain and it plumps back up and fills up again. The continued stress on the structure of the ball of clay or the earth will cause an earthquake effect in the earth or a pit or breaking up of the ball of clay. So it is with sin, Sin causes wars because of greed or power. Famines are caused because of greed and lack of responsibility for caring for the earth and God's people. You cannot blame God for man's sin.

Is Jesus Really the Only Way?

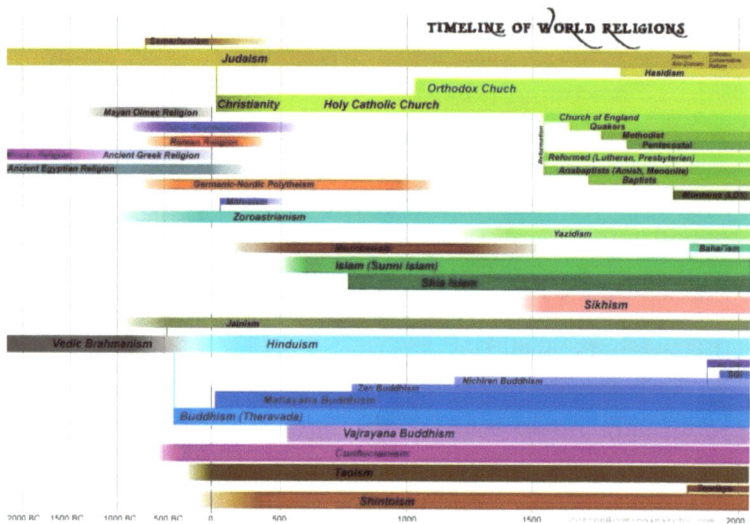

Is Jesus Really the Only Way? Scripture tells us in John 14:6 that "Jesus saith unto him; I am the way, the truth and the life; No man cometh unto the Father, but by me". Christianity is not just the only exclusive religion. There are many other exclusive religions including Buddha and Mohammad in the world that say their way is the right way.

Some religions go to the extreme to make their belief system the only one with the majority members. It is just that Christianity is the only one whereby Jesus is actually showing up in divine revelations by dreams and other revelatory ways to prove that He is the way, the truth and the life. Some in the Muslim culture have been coming forward and saying that Jesus appeared to them and told them that HE is the truth and that they should follow HIM.

I know from firsthand experience that HIS way is truth and that HE is alive and that is a personal statement and account that I can give that HE is the way, the truth and the life. He is the only way that my prayers get to the Father. He is my only entrance to the Father. When God the father sees me, HE sees Jesus because Jesus' blood has paid for my sins and now I can freely go to the Father in prayer through Jesus and get my petitions heard and answered by the One and only true God of the universe.

The key to salvation is that you have to continue to seek God until you find HIM. I went to the alter at age 12 in a Methodist church and I said the salvation prayer that they lead me in. Nothing happened. I don't know why. My first boyfriend in the sixth grade was my next door neighbor whose father was a preacher. He was my first boyfriend and he was the son of a preacher man, but once more that didn't help me when they took me to their Nazarene church. And again later while I was in my early twenties I took my two young children to church and I went forward to be baptized at a Baptist church. Again, nothing happened.

It was only when I was pregnant with my third child that I was desperate for answers. I didn't believe in divorce from as long as I could remember. I hated divorce! But after two years of marriage counseling that my first husband refused to go to and after seven and a half years of emotional and physical abuse my mother lead me away from him when I told her that the marriage counselor suspected that my ex-husband was abusing my children.

So I remarried less than three years after our divorce. During my pregnancy I caught him cheating on me in the worst way possible--he was sleeping with anything that had legs! A lady saw me walking home from the store one evening in my 7th month of pregnancy. She mistook me for a friend of hers from church. She stopped and asked if she could give me a ride. I accepted and on the way home she asked me if she could pray for me about anything and then she asked me if I would like to ride with her to church in the morning.

My husband had gone deer hunting as he did occasionally in Vicksburg, MS. where his folks had a big farm, a family operated store and pool hall and he had a lot of brothers and friends there. When he would go he would always stay gone the entire weekend because it was a few hours' drive from Richland, MS. where we lived. And his family was very busy on the weekends with the pool hall and alcohol sales.

When she prayed she started using a heavenly language known as tongues. My mother had always warned me to stay away from any tongue talkers because she said the devil would come after me. Well, I didn't have much of a choice. My mother was nowhere around and I was desperate! I asked the lady to pray for my husband to come home. It was a Saturday night and I knew my husband would not be home until Monday.

Unbeknownst to me my ex-husband comes rolling in a 2AM and throws a deer in the front yard. The next morning the kids and I got up and went to church. Once more when the alter call was given I asked Jesus to save me. That morning in church service I saw everyone raising their hands and praising the Lord so I decided I would try to do the same. When I did that something in my heart changed greatly! I had surrendered to God! I let down all my guards! I had always been very proud and kind of self-centered egotistically. When I took myself off the pedestal of my heart and I put Jesus there I had a heart transformation.

That night, I got baptized "In Jesus Name" my life was so radically changed from that day on. What I once thought true my whole life, I learned was a lie. And I learned that one was not supposed to be a taker in life but that it was exactly opposite. That we are to be givers and even helpers. Not just to stop cheating, lying or stealing to get ahead or to survive. But to actually START and BEGIN to give money away to God, and to the poor. What a radical change in my heart and life that was.

I also learned that I didn't have to depend on my husband or myself, I didn't have to depend on my parents or on anyone but now I had someone that I really could actually trust. Someone who would be there for me day or night. Someone who would never leave me or forsake me, cheat on me or reject me. I now could lean on someone else besides myself. I no longer had to depend on my own self to solve every problem in life.

A year and a half later, I began learning about tithing from a great faith teacher Pastor Robert Tilton and I have never stopped tithing since those early years. Tithing is when you give 10% of all your income to the Lord. I also give alms to the poor, and I keep the three HOLY feasts offerings as was taught to me by Pastor Steve Munsey. I've been doing that since Spring or Passover of 2000.

Later, I learned that I was not to put myself ahead of others but to esteem everyone else ahead of myself. To prefer others before myself. Some of the bible principals were easier at the beginning then they were at other times in my life after long periods of trials or tribulation, injustices or even persecutions. But still, it was a whole new way of thinking for me after I was born again. Salvation is real!

Reality of the Sin Condition In Church

& The Afterlife

It is sad and hard for me to face the reality regarding sin in the church. But I can tell you that God does chasten those HE loves. I was saved in 1988 but I never knew anything but the old sinful lifestyle as I was not raised in a Christian home. The Christian lifestyle was a huge change for me. I stayed backslid like a dog to it's vomit on and off for almost five years.

Now, I've been walking strong for the Lord under extremely difficult circumstances for 14 years when most others would have compromised. God will separate the wheat from the tares one day. Just keep your eyes on HIM and not on man.

As far as being anything after death on earth, can you imagine how empty that would feel if earth was all there was to life? How desolate, useless and helpless that would make one feel if there was nothing after life on earth? Do you think if a person finds their purpose in life, the one thing that they know they were created for that would help them to consider the afterlife?

Critical Thinking (Footnotes Included)

Critical Thinking

Secular Humanism Worldview

Worldview for Secular Humanism concerning origin would say that natural existence that has always been has brought about their being and existence. That all matter in the universe has always been and that they came into existence as a time and chance occurred. Worldview on the identity from a Secular Humanistic thought is very sad in that they think they have no real value other than that of the value of an animal. They think that animals and humans have the same value and that they just exist and that is how it has always been. Mere existence is their central thought towards all life forms and that is the only identity for Secular Humanism.

Purpose and life meaning for Secular Humanism would be not much more than some temporary substance that they would pass on to the next generation. If they were able to gain any knowledge, wisdom or monetary value in this lifetime that it would simply be donated or taught to the next generation that would remain after they were deceased. They would simply teach other students what they learn and pass down the information gained or they would leave a donation to a particular cause that they felt worthy.

The scariest part of a Secular Humanist world view is the question of morality. They simply have no moral conscious at all. A Secular Humanist has the scariest of all religious worldview moral outlooks. To not think one has any boundaries or limits on the actions of one's life is an extremely dangerous threat to any populace or society.

The final destiny of the life of a Secular Humanist would be nothing more than to just simply die off. There is no afterlife for a Secular Humanist. After death then life is completely over for them. They think that they just rot and decay upon the moment of death and that is it.

Christian Worldview

Origin for A Christian is found in Genesis. God created man from dust. Eve formed from Adam's rib and created from the bone of his rib. We were from and created by God. HE knit us together in our mother's womb. Eve was the mother of all human life. God created Eve from Adam's rib. As opposed to a Secular Humanistic Worldview on Origin who just came about as a matter of time and chance.

Identity for a Christian is one held in awe and esteemed with honor among all creation. As we are God's special creation in that we are uniquely created to have fellowship with God and we are the only creation that HE made in HIS image. HE even esteems us higher than all the heavenly hosts of angels. Our Identity for Christians is in Christ Jesus. It is no longer I that lives but Christ Jesus who lives through me. In contrast with a Humanistic Worldview on Identity who think they are nothing more than just another form of life.

Purpose and Meaning in life for the Christian is much influenced by the word of God. It reflects how one would vote on an election where abortion were an issue or where traditional marriage values were an issue. And our purpose is to become like Christ, to live as HE would have us to live, do what HE would have us to do, become what HE would have us to become. Our purpose and meaning would revolve around Christ Jesus. Christians have significant purpose in life but it is so sad for the Secular Humanist who believe they are of no real significance on earth other than any knowledge or monetary value that they can leave behind after they die.

Our moral values are influenced primarily by the word of God. What God esteems and honors is what a Christian should esteem and honor. What God detests and abhors then we should detest and abhor. The word of God should become the foundation for our thoughts and our conscious. If God calls it sin then we too should acknowledge it as sin. We are to be Holy as HE is holy.

 We are to love and honor HIS word and keep HIS commandments. Christians are people who one can generally feel safe around because you have a sense that they can be trusted since they are accountable to God for their actions. On the other hand it is very hard to think about leaving a child that you love with a Secular Humanistic person who has no sense of right or wrong and has no conscious either.

Our destiny upon our death for the Christian may seem sad at first but when you realize there will be no more persecution for that soul who dwelt in an earthen vessel, there will be no more sorrow for that man of God or woman of God, for that Christian but only a life spent in Heaven with our Savior and Lord who they have spent their Christian lives adoring. For the Christian who dies it is nothing but sweet relief. The Secular Humanist believe that life is all that there is for them and that upon death there is nothing else.

Genesis 2:7
Hebrews 2:7
Genesis 1:27
1 Corinthians 11:1
Galatians 2:20
1 Peter 1:15-17

Judaism Was Here Hundreds of Years Before Islāmic Religion

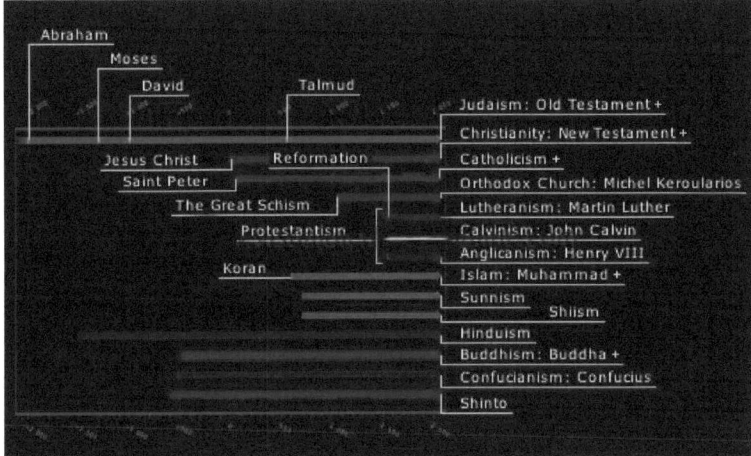

We should be very wise in the way that we evangelize. Actions speak louder than words and they don't necessarily have to be direct interactions with other people but our lifestyles in and of themselves speaks volumes to even people we've never even met.

One thing that I've just learned because of last week is that Muslims believe Christians and Jews have desecrated the Qur'an and I was thrilled to learn that on the World Religion Time Line that we studied at the first of this subterm taught us that Hinduism was the oldest religion and that Judaism came along before Islāmic Religion.

This means that our Holy Bible has not desecrated their text in the Qur'an and the Hadith but all of our historical Dead Sea scrolls and even the Holy Masoretic manuscripts date back to A.D. 900.

And unless they can prove that their Qur'an and Hadith

were written before our oldest Holy texts then that means that Surah 2:75 78-79 can be challenged as their truth that they use to accuse the Jews and Christians of sabotaging the Qur'an.

I once had a friend from Iraq. We worked together at El Palacios Mexican restaurant in Jackson, MS. in the mid-eighties. He was a very nice guy and we wanted so much to accept each other that he told me that Allah was one and the same as the God that I serve.

My heart and spirit knew differently even way back then. But it never stopped us from being the dearest of friends. Things are a bit different now and I am not sure that I would feel as comfortable in that relationship today.

Judaism Was Here Before Islamic Religion

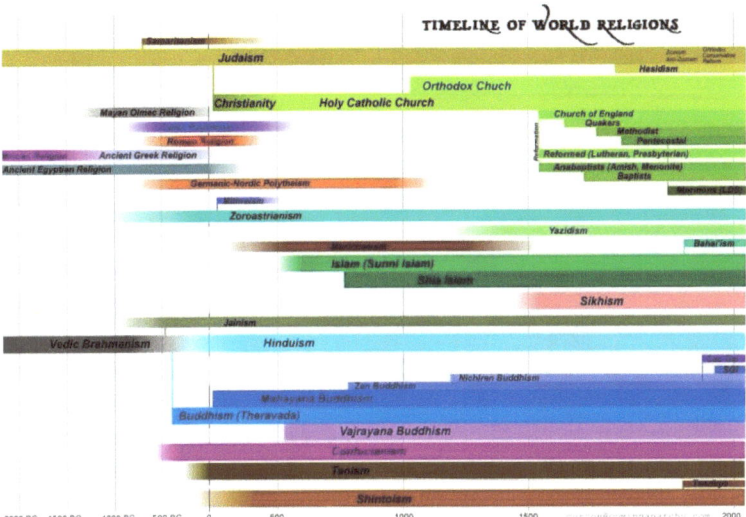

Islamic Religion wasn't even here when Judaism came to play a big role on the world timeline of Religion that dates back hundreds of years before Muhammad had even been thought of. Yet, Islamic Religion says in the Surah 2:75 78-79 that Jews and Christians have desecrated their Holy text.

However we should consider to date their Holy Text that Muhammad wrote in the Qur'an and Hadith in comparison with our Holy Text Dead Sea Scrolls and with our Masoretic manuscripts that date back to A.D. 900.
The Holy Virgin Mother Mary and the ridicule that her husband Joseph went through even though he was innocent is another point that they cannot argue.

Or the fact that Jesus was crucified, died and was buried in a rich man's tomb but HE rose again with all the witnesses and officials that gave testimony and account of that is another point that they cannot argue with.

The Spirit of the Lord has been witnessing and drawing lots of Muslim's unto the Lord for the last decade and they certainly cannot challenge HIS validity either because HE personalizes HIS presence individually to each and every one that HE draws to HIMSELF.

If It Isn't Yours Then Don't Touch It; ISRAEL

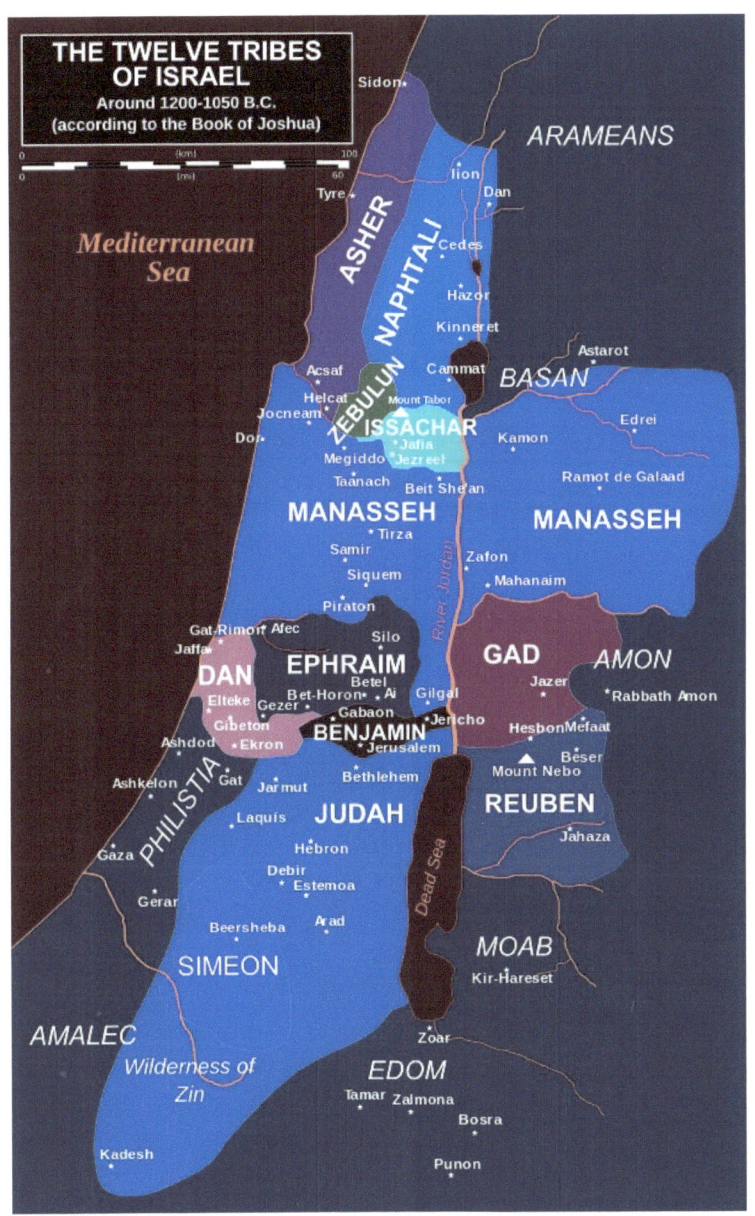

Islam spread through violence throughout the years because of what the Qur'an says

Surah 2:191, 4:89 Unbelievers are to be killed (everywhere you find them)

Surah 9:123 Fight unbeliever who are near

Surah 8:12 Strike of the heads and fingertips of those who disbelieve

Surah 9:5 Slay idolators wherever you find them

Surah 4:11-12 Women do not have the right to inheritance

Surah 4:34 Husbands have the right to beat disobedient wives

The historical Bible inheritance and division of the Holy Land by God that HE gave to HIS holy people Israel included the territory from the land of Egypt to the river Euphrates Genesis 15:18. The current nation of Israel possesses but a fragment of that land.

Because the Arabs think that Ismael the illegitimate son of Abraham to Sara's handmaiden Islam claims that the land should belong to Ismael (first born and all of his decedent) but God specifically told Abraham that HE wanted Issac to be the recipient of the first born promise.

So the battle between the issues of inheritance for Ishmael (Islam) or Isaac (Judaism and Christianity) have continued throughout hundreds of years. Because of that the former Israeli Prime Minister Golda Meir "We will have peace with the Arabs when they love their children more than they hate us."

World leaders from the Western hemisphere have no business dividing land that they have no inheritance or part in. It is none of their business and it never has been. It is a fatal mistake to rule from any place of authority without the basic knowledge of all world religions. You wouldn't want to fall into the hands of an angry God now would you?

5 Main Themes Of San Diego Metropolitan Geography

San Diego Metropolitan
Reflections Essay
Kimmy Nelson

The Five Main Themes of geography of San Diego and her
suburban city of La Mesa
1.   Location –Latitude and Longitude
2.   Place –What is it like there
3.   Movement –People, Ideas, Goods moving from one place to
another
4.   Region—A Group Of Places that have any human or
physical characteristics in common
5. Human Environmental Interaction—Humans Adapt To
Environment or Effect The Environment

Five Themes Of Geography For San Diego and Her Suburban City of La Mesa

Location

San Diego Metropolitan Area

The port of San Diego, CA. is home to our navy is Latitude, 32°44'8" North and Longitude, 117°10'36" West. The Chargers play at Qualcomm Stadium which has it's own Trolley exit called "Qualcomm Stadium" headquartered in Chargers Park. San Diego, CA. is in the South--Western Hemisphere of The United States of America. San Diego is a border city as it is on the Northern border of Mexico on the West Coast in America. La Mesa, CA. is only a ten miles North East of San Diego, CA.

Place

Southern California

San Diego and her suburb city of La Mesa, CA. are some of the finest areas that Southern California has to offer. San Diego is the home of the National Football Team the San Diego Chargers. San Diego is also home to the United States Navy since 1918 with 54 ships and 13 piers. The Chargers moved to San Diego in 1961 and in 1970 they had the AFL-NFL merger after winning the AFC four times.

Movement

Distribution and Mobility

We have the best public transportation system that anyone could ever hope for with the Metropolitan Transit System of buses, trains and trolleys that are all connected at many different locations and times throughout the regions of San

Diego and her suburban areas. There are also boats and shipping vessels all along the bay and port areas along the coastal shores and waterways. There is also a ferry that will carry your vehicle across the water. San Diego has a huge airport where many people fly to as it is the main airport South of Los Angeles, CA. Pedestrians and bikers travel along the sidewalks and roads throughout San Diego and La Mesa too.

Culture & Surroundings

In 2012 the statistics from the San Diego County Census Bureau reported that the White population to be 76.6% and that the black or African American population to be 5.6% while the Native American Indian were only 1.3% in population. The Asian population was 11.6% of the population and Hawaiian and other Pacific Islanders were only .06% of the population.

Two or more races present in the households were 4.2%. Hispanic was 32.7% in population and the White alone not Hispanic or Latino were 47.6% in population. While 49.7% are female in gender, less than 6.7% are children under five years old and less than 23% are teenagers under eighteen years of age.
And 12% are 65 years of age or older male or females living in San Diego County. 83% have lived in the same house for over one year 2008-2012. 23.2% are foreign born persons 2008-2012 and 37.1% use another language where they reside other than English 2008-2012.

85.4% are High School Graduates 2008-2012, 34% have a Bachelor's Degree between 2008-2012 and over 230, 000 Veterans between 2008 and 2012. 54.5% home ownership 2008-2012 and approximately $30, 683.00 per capita in the past twelve months 2008-2012.

As you can see we are a very diverse culture with a lot to offer. And as one of the world's top twelve highest earning agriculture environments is all the more reason why it is a very important global region.

And even with the statistics previously mentioned there are still 13.9% of our population that are listed as below poverty income between 2008 and 2012. In 2008 the city of San Diego was reported to be one of the top ten safest cities with populations over 100,000 persons. In 2010 the city of San Diego was listed as one of the top ten highest crime and unsafe cities with populations over 100,000 persons.

This could be attributed to the drug war crossing over into America from Mexico. I believe that our local government is as much responsible for our border security as the Federal government because no one cares about their own neighborhood as much as the person who lives there.

The Federal government in large does not have to deal with having their purse stole, their identity stole or a violent gang member who is lawless. Nor do they have to worry about the gang member who watches to see when you leave your home so that they can illegally enter at their own liberty.

We have a rich military history here in San Diego with the navy using our ports as home base. And the military have a wonderful community nearby the ports where they have their own little close knit communities of mothers and children and wives or spouses of our United States Military.

Region

Climate

The climate here is somewhat tropical throughout Southern California so it is lush with green shrubs, ivy, and beautiful flowers scattered throughout like a tapestry landscape in between the buildings and the highways. There are also lots of avocado farms, orange groves, almond trees, and grape vines where large quantities of fruits and vegetables are grown and harvested annually as San Diego is home to the twelfth largest crop producing area in our state. The entire Region South of Los Angeles share the same climate and temperature on a daily basis. There are occasional winds and sometimes there are droughts. We have occasional earthquakes throughout the entire region of California but it is our climate that separates us from the rest of the state. As San Diego has perfect temperatures all year round that is suitable for human life and sustainability.

Human Environmental Interactions

Transportation and Architecture

Fishing boats, fisheries and lots of seafood restaurants that are connected to the seafood industry have had quite an impact on the sea life environment. The freeways, interstates, railroad tracks and buildings in mass numbers in this dense population have also had a great effect on the environment making everything much more accessible.

Earth's Dynamics

The earthquake prone tectonic plates, the fire prone mountains and forests along with the mudslide prone hills in the San Diego area have also had an effect on the way that people build businesses and homes and even the way that insurance is sold or distributed because they must take in considerations those likely scenarios before they can build or issue an insurance policy.

Green House Gas Emissions

The green house gases and ocean pollution have now caught the attention of the world as to how vitally important the coral reefs are to human survival so that there are now some efforts to clean up the mess that we've made. Just off the coast of San Diego there is a Plastic Vortex floating that is the size of two states of Texas where plastic hovers above the oceans surface on the waves and even beneath the surface a few feet deep. It is disposed garbage that somehow found its way to the ocean and has polluted and killed much of the ocean life. Some are working on solutions how to clean it up and prevent it from happening again.

References

1. http://quickfacts.census.gov/qfd/states/06/06073.html

2. http://geography.about.com/od/teachgeography/a/5themes.htm

3. http://en.wikipedia.org/wiki/Plate_tectonics

4. http://en.wikipedia.org/wiki/Great_Pacific_garbage_patch

www.ingramcontent.com/pod-product-compliance
Lightning Source LLC
Chambersburg PA
CBHW050904290526
45792CB00002B/698